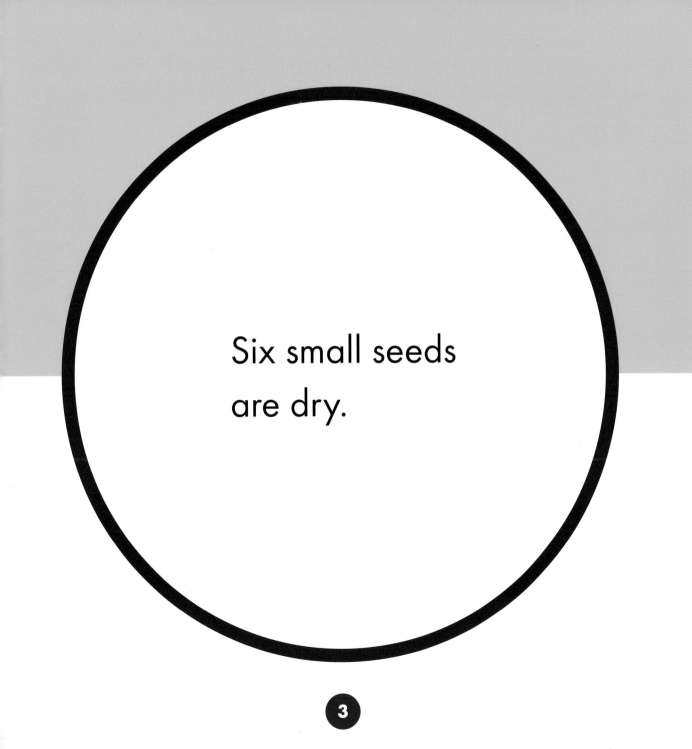

Six small seeds
are dry.

Six small seeds
go in the ground.

Six small seeds
get covered up.

Six small seeds
need water.

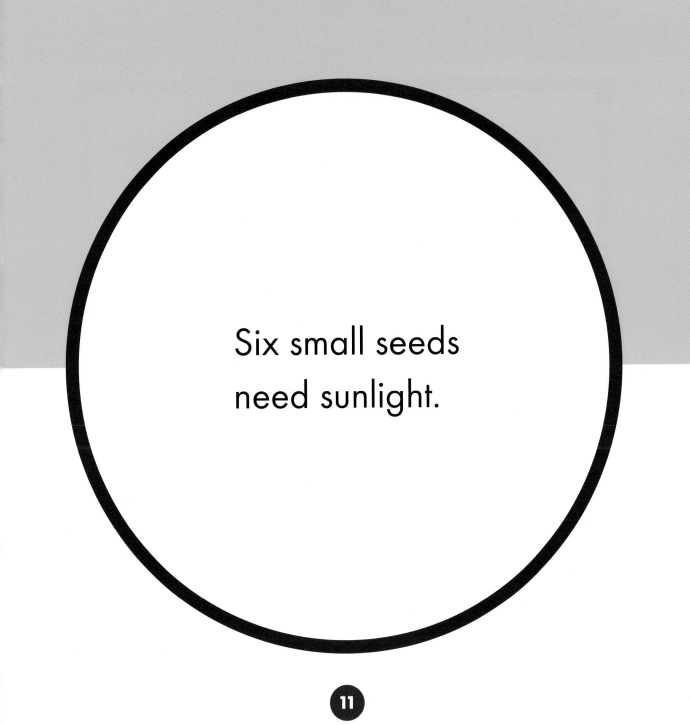

Six small seeds
need sunlight.

Six small seeds
start to grow.

Six small seeds
grow roots.

Six small seeds
begin to grow up.

Six small seeds
grow leaves.

Six small seeds
will be flowers!

Note to Caregivers and Educators

Sight words are a foundation for reading. It's important for young readers to have sight words memorized at a glance without breaking them down into individual letter sounds. Sight words are often phonetically irregular and can't be sounded out, so readers need to memorize them. Knowing sight words allows readers to focus on more difficult words in the text. The intent of this book is to repeat specific sight words as many times as possible throughout the story. Through repetition of the words, emerging readers will recognize, and ideally memorize, each sight word. Memorizing sight words can help improve readers' literacy skills.

seeds

six

small

About the Author

Tora Stephenchel lives in
Minnesota. She loves to spend
time with her son, daughter,
husband, and two silly dogs.

The Child's World®
childsworld.com

Published by The Child's World®
1980 Lookout Drive • Mankato, MN 56003-1705
800-599-READ • www.childsworld.com

Photographs © amenic181/Shutterstock.com: 5; Big Foot Productions/Shutterstock.com: cover, 1,
2; Bloom/Shutterstock.com: 21; Bogdan Wankowicz/Shutterstock.com: 13, 14, 17; Budimir Jevtic/
Shutterstock.com: 18; Chatchawal Kittirojana/Shutterstock.com: 23; Naypong Studio/Shutterstock.
com: 9; sumroeng chinnapan/Shutterstock.com: 10; Wstockstudio/Shutterstock.com: 6

ISBN 9781503845022 (Reinforced Library Binding)
ISBN 9781503846586 (Portable Document Format)
ISBN 9781503847774 (Online Multi-user eBook)
LCCN: 2020931096

Printed in the United States of America